The Cosmos of the Heart

Marguerite Guzmán Bouvard

Art is about aesthetics, about morals,
about our belief in humanity.
Without that there is simply no art

Ai Weiwei

ACKNOWLEDGEMENTS

With gratitude to the magazines in which these poems first appeared,

- *Liu Xiaobo, There are Stories,* Tuck Magazine for Human Rights
- *Behind the Shadows,* Tell Tale Inklings
- *Anything is Possible, Ceremonies, Both, Question,* Unlikely Stories IV &V&VI
- *The Light Inside and Outside, Danny Rodriguez, The Last Word, Perspectives,* Evening Street Press
- *The Music of Our Daily Lives, winner of 22nd Moon Prize, The Magician, Rites of Passage, Meeting in West Maui, Pesira, Power, Marking America Great Again, For giveness,* Writing in a Woman's Voice
- *An Invisible Community of Love and Caring, Inter twined,* New Verse News
- *New York City,* Soft Cartel
- *A Lost Art, Vertigo, Two Worlds,* Ethos Literary Magazine
- *Michelle Obama, Dimensions, Small Miracles,* Pangolin Review
- *Perspectives,* Kingdom in the Wild
- *Geshe, Look Above Us, featured with two of her poetry books in November 2018,* Blue Heron Press
- *In A Secluded Cove,* Somerville Lyrical
- *A Dream of Order, Becoming New,* Eunoia Review
- *Neighbors, Earth's Scriptures,* Kerf
- *Another Way of Seeing, Diagnosis,* Soaring Without Limits
- *In Only One Night, Just Words,* Colere
- *Ariel, No Words,* Trajectory
- *Lessons,* Chest Magazine
- *Goya's Portrait,* Sunlight Review

Published by Human Error Publishing
Paul Richmond
www.humanerrorpublishing.com
paul@humanerrorpublishing.com

Copyright © 2020
by
Human Error Publishing
&
Marguerite Guzmán Bouvard

All Rights Reserved

ISBN: 978-1-948521-47-5

Front Cover:
&
Back Cover
by
Jacques Bouvard

TABLE OF CONTENTS

The Oneness of Our Humanity 10

Liu Xiaobo 11
Wu Qiang 12
There Are Stories 13
Behind The Shadows 14
Power 15
The Light Inside And Outside 16
The Music Of Our Daily Lives 17
An Invisible Community Of Love And Caring 18
New York City 19
Vertigo 21
The Magician 22
Danny Rodriguez 23
The World 24
A Lost Art 25
Michelle Obama 27
Rites Of Passage 28
Question 29
Ceremonies 30
The Way Of Our Continuing 31
Both 32
Forgiveness 33
The Last Word 34
Goya's Etchings 35
Geshe 36
Faith 37

The Earth's Scriptures 38

Voices 39
The Emperor's Forbidden City 40
In A Secluded Cove 41
Perspectives 42
Meeting In West Maui 43
Small Miracles 44

Look Above Us 45

Neighbors 46

Becoming New 47

Despite Us 48

Dawn On A Faraway Island 49

A Dream Of Order 50

There Was Once A Sea 51

Simultaneously 52

The Importance Of Flowers 53

Harmony 54

Earth's Scriptures 55

Dimensions 56

The Thermal Park At Le Fayet 57

Two Worlds 58

Perception 59

WHERE EVERYTHING HAPPENS 60

Paris 61

Behind The Church 62

La Route De Maison Neuve 63

Letter To My Daughter 64

Ariel 65

Goya's Portrait 66

Unspoken 67

No Words 68

Just Words 69

In Only One Night 70

Lessons 71

Diagnosis 72

Moments 73

Pesira 74

Two Make One 75

Another Way 76

Autumn 77

A Different Way Of Seeing 78

The Gift 80

The Book Of Lights 81

The Oneness of Our Humanity

LIU XIAOBO

Returning from his studies at Columbia University
because he loved his country, he led
the 1989 Tiananmen Square Democracy movement
and cajoled the students to retreat, to stay alive,
when the army opened fire, then hauled him off

to prison, courage continually blossoming
in his heart, for this was just the beginning of his life's
work, and imprisonment. Yet there was a land within him
where justice reigned. In 2008 he was arrested yet again,
for his efforts on behalf of the rule of law and an end

to censorship. He remained incarcerated, separated
from a wife he cherished, for whom he wrote poems,
when he won the Nobel Prize for his endless struggles
on behalf of Democracy, and he warned
an enemy mentality can destroy a society's tolerance

and humanity, at a time when populism flourished
in the West and "fake news" was rampant in our country,
and the word "we" crumbled in the battles between "us"
and "them," where hatred defaced mosques and Jewish
cemeteries were defiled, and in a Kansas bar, an engineer,

Srinivas Kuchibhotla, was confronted with angry slurs
and shot to death -- while Liu Xiaobo was suffering
from liver cancer insisting that he did not see
his prison guards as enemies, even though
he was not allowed to leave for proper medical care,

for in the darkness of his confinement, his soul
was illuminated. After he died, his lessons
and his life's efforts remain timeless; that there is neither
East or West, that we all need to honor compromise,
and moderation, the oneness of our humanity.

WU QIANG

a dissident, drove 400 miles
from Beijing to Shenyang
to be near Liu Xiaobo in his
final days, and then held not only
his grief, but the eloquent silence
he did not expect from Western
governments, especially the U.S.
that seemed more concerned
with trade, but he moved beyond
the despair and isolation of his fellow
dissidents, the censoring of online
tributes, telling them through foreign
newspapers, on one side is darkness
on the other is hope.

THERE ARE STORIES

we turn away from when we would like
to have a glass of wine over a quiet table,
make a list of the week's coming events.
We would like to be safe in world that continues
to defy us. But the world has its own

voices. After World War II, there was a trial
in Germany that captured our attention,
while members of the SS quietly
slipped away across borders and remained
anonymous. There are always trials, the ones

that take place in courts, and the trials
we live through when clouds bring
us heavy rain, the tears rolling under
our eyelids, when the defector from Syria
who slipped out with documents depicting

the thousands of prisoners that perished
in Bashar al-Assad's prisons, and then stood
before the powerful in our country with his
photographs, telling them, *My life is not more
valuable than the many who are being killed*

*inside the country. I died a hundred times
a day, and looking at these bodies broke
my heart* -- he who embraced the world
that thunders towards us with his open arms,
telling us that the darkness must never win.

BEHIND THE SHADOWS

There are wars raging across the world,
newspaper headlines blare,
and a young man wrote an article
about charity, telling us that photos

of sad children in refugee camps
do not speak to us, that we need to use
faces that show accomplishments
to inspire giving. But there is a quiet world

that vibrates behind the shadows;
during a famine a little girl shares
her only piece of bread, another person
embraces a child who lost

his father, and yet another has given
a veteran a trained dog to help him
with his trauma, each gesture reaching
beyond oneself, and quietly from the wisdom

of the heart, creates a new way of living,
a knowledge that defies the darkness.

POWER

for Colin Kaepernick

1

We walk into a protected natural reserve
for native Hawai'ians,
a narrow path between trees and boulders with the sound
of the distant surf, then come upon a blond woman
in an electric cart. When she sees the surprise
on my face, she says, We own this,
the ranch up the mountain.

2

There is a mirror where only one image
flickers with its own colors and shades
and there is only one language only
one way to honor the Creator.

3

The football player kneels during
the national anthem, kneeling to honor
his soul to honor social justice and the color
of his skin that too many disdain.

THE LIGHT INSIDE AND OUTSIDE
Gerhard Ter Borch, The knife grinders family

Open windows and an open door
are filled with darkness, not like
the brick wall that is aged and in ruins
but pulsing with light, and the courtyard

is where life happens, the father
working in a corner sharpening knives
and the mother seated on a chair
with her daughter leaning her head

on her lap so she can remove
the lice from her hair, broken
chairs in full view-- is where the poor
are celebrated by artists in past centuries,

but today there are no painters
who capture the light and color
of daily life in an inner city neighborhood,
on corners or on the sidewalks

or where the darkness spreads
its mantle while Eric Garner
is selling cigarettes to make a living
on a crowded city street

only to be ambushed by the police
and held in a chokehold until
he died. Today, the pieces of truth that
we live with are captured

by cell phones of passersby
and bystanders, by ordinary
people who can pierce the darkness
with the flick of a finger.

THE MUSIC OF OUR DAILY LIVES

The leaves on the birch tree
are singing in the wind, a melody
with its own rise and fall of notes,

and in the distance a child's voice at play
reminds us to live in the moment.
There are so many different melodies

in our lives, the lies that are tailored
to divert attention and turn our minds
to smoke, with right and wrong

continually changing their notes,
without any transparency of words
in speeches. There are so many different

melodies in our lives, a mother's reassuring,
voice, the harsh words that wound us,
for we all carry wounds, like the Somali boy

who was threatened with deportation
and trekked for days to Canada, carrying
the voices of his parents who were

slaughtered in Somali, his fatigue making him
collapse on the frozen ground,
until a Canadian border guard lifted him

up in his arms, and assured him that he could stay
-- the music in the cosmos of our hearts,
that uplifts us, and cannot be silenced.

AN INVISIBLE COMMUNITY OF LOVE AND CARING

thrived around a grate on 46th street in New York City,
where people hurry past to their destinations. Nakesha,
a brilliant and promising student whose life spiraled
into homelessness because of mental problems
made this grate her dominion. Surrounded by a cart,

bags of clothing, books and papers, she read
Anna Karenina, The War of Worlds, and wrote letters,
refusing to stay in homeless shelters, because she knew
they were unsafe or to accept medical care because
she didn't want to be labeled. But there were people who

passed by and became her friends. P.J. who brought
her toiletries, a raincoat, leather boots, and underwear.
A street vendor, a Moroccan immigrant, who parked
his coffee cart near the grate made her a breakfast
of eggs, a bun and cranberry juice, and protected her

from a man who taunted her, blocked another one
from stealing her purse. Another vendor,
an Egyptian immigrant who operated a sandwich cart
prepared her favorite lunch, chicken and rice. An optician
who passed by left her small gifts, hand lotion,

socks, and sneakers. When Nakasha died, P.J. knew
that her body would have been buried with unclaimed bodies
in a mass grave, and so she had her cremated, placing her ashes
in a mother of pearl urn flecked with gold. An office worker who
learned of P.J.'s efforts collected donations
for the funeral

service and sent P.J. an envelope with money
and 21 signatures. Nakasha's college friends
gathered at the grate and lit candles for
her memorial service, reminding us of the
light that too many pass by.

NEW YORK CITY

At first I stared through the 12th floor
window at the cement high rises,
their windows identical, the sky cancelled
by their height, wishing for a green leaf.
But it was Uber that unexpectedly
thrilled me. On my first ride,

the driver spoke Hungarian and
we chatted about my friend who was among
the first to flee the communist regime,
and about Victor Orban the new leader
whom I disliked because he leaned
towards Russia, learning from

the driver, the depth of corruption
in Hungary, the poverty of its ordinary
people. Then there was the driver
from China and I listened to his radio
station in Mandarin, remembering
my time working with Lao refugees

when my attempt to speak a tonal
language made them burst into
laughter. The driver with the long beard
and a high round hat that seemed
from the middle ages, told me that
he spoke Bengali, and I answered
that my Pakistani friend spoke Urdu,

but he replied that everyone there
spoke Bengali. And the driver from
Afghanistan told me that he came here
because of Russia's war there, and that now
it was Pakistan that was the problem,

and I answered that I knew its army was
protecting the Haqqani rebels and others
on the borders. Finally instead of the usual

blast of pop music, I heard the classical
music I love and learned that the young man's
wife was studying for a career in music,

and he thanked me for my questions
with a lovely Latin American accent.
So I toured the world, not as a diplomat
with his government's message, or a traveler
on a luxurious cruise, but meeting people who
hold their country's history in their daily lives.

VERTIGO

The falcon soars far above us,
a denizen of light and air
circling different wind currents
in a vastness that eludes us

until he sees the smallest speck,
a rabbit emerging from its hole,
and he zooms down to capture it
in less than a minute -- like the vertigo

of parachuting words on the pages of life
as Zahur Ahmad Zindani who lost
his eyesight, and his father
from a bombing, walks on a march

he founded for peace to Kabul,
for forty nights and forty days,
400 miles under a burning sky,
under the night-sorrow of memory

and the day-sorrow of the war
torn road, reciting his poetry
for his lost love, *my eyes did not
shut waiting for you.*

THE MAGICIAN

We are surrounded by a cold fog,
not just in the mountains,
but in our country where the facts
are turned upside down, where ordinary

citizens become scapegoats, and a woman
in a restaurant screams at a woman
on another table for wearing a headscarf.
The fog obliterates our vision, shelters

anger and the man who waves his wand
everywhere like a magician pulling
tricks out of his hat and the crowd that
applauds for he will provide jobs

for everyone, make our country
strong, provide security, and bypass
institutions the crowds believe no longer
serve us while the political parties

disagree among and within themselves
and like Weimar the crowds believe
the magician will push aside the "elite"
and solve all of their problems.

DANNY RODRIGUEZ

7:00 o'clock.
The light is getting dim.
You are waiting for the door
to open, to hear your daddy's
voice, asking you how your day
went, to feel his arms
holding you. He will read you
the stories you hear at bedtime
every night. But this time after
he came in, another door
opened. A man entered who is
a ICE* official, was an angry face
whom you've never seen before.
He grabbed your father and dragged
him away. You cannot sleep,
and when you do, you scream.
You have no words, so you just
throw your breakfast on the floor,
and pull you hair. You have no
answers. The door doesn't open
when the light dims, although
you listen. Your home is strange.
When the light dims, you are
so afraid. You have no words,
the air is empty.

(*) Immigration and Customs Enforcement

THE WORLD

is small. There is the internet,
iPhones, and FaceTime. The world
is small because it lives
in my heart, like the four months old
baby ripped from his father's

arms at the border and shipped
to an unknown destination.
His father sobs for there are no
words that can explain
or describe his situation, no daylight.

He took a journey with his wife
and baby because he believed
in possibilities, that as a Roma
he would no longer be mocked
and mistreated in the country

where he was born and didn't
belong. Are we so busy with our
jobs and our daily lives that we
have no time or interest in these
events and live behind closed

doors. I spoke to an English woman
about Brexit when we were
in France, but she replied
that the news was tedious,
and changed the subject because

she wanted to enjoy herself.
But we all have hearts, and they
can be very strong with open doors,
and room upon room where people
can feel safe and understood.

A LOST ART
for Annalisa Spoljaric

There is the blong of cowbells, the insects
buzzing in the high heat. Yet we have lost
the art of listening to each other

as a woman tells the story of her days
to a person who may look at her,
but is turning inward to her own thoughts.

Then there are the children who were separated
from their families at our border,
sobbing while the guard who surveys

the prison where they are held grins
and comments there should be a conductor
for these sounds. There are so many languages

and tones. Some break the threads that bind us,
turning away a boat filled with migrants.
But in a corner of Trieste there is a woman

who teaches the refugees Italian and opens up
her life where there are no strangers
as she listens to Rosa from the Congo

who recounts the atrocities
in her village, Addis, a child bride
and illiterate, left her five children behind

as she escaped the violence in Ethiopia.
This woman who spends her time
listening with kindness to a long list

of heartfelt stories is a friend to poverty, grief,
and tragedy, considers the refugees
as sisters, and as a grandmother to a tiny

Nigerian boy who giggles before her with laughter
in his eyes, as they celebrate our diversity
shining a light on a troubled world.

MICHELLE OBAMA

She is beautiful and intelligent,
well versed in law. But while shopping
at Target, a worker tells her
"Put those boxes on the shelf!"
The mirror is opaque: she's been
featured on the cover of Vogue,
so people rush to buy the clothes
similar to the ones she is wearing, forgetting
for a moment the definitions
that were made long ago, but are still sharp
and direct as knives. Our country
has constructed boundaries
that some people cannot cross
and they are everywhere, visible
only to those who have been defined.
Although surrounded by people
who have standing and the grounds
where she lives are in public view,
she has planted a vegetable garden
because she sees what so many
are oblivious of as they hurry through
their own lives and concerns, that children
who are poor need healthy meals.
Her life is a story that has many
chapters: her inner light, and wisdom,
the accomplishments that are
not applauded, the phrases she hears
that are flung arrows. What would you do
if she rang your doorbell in the evening?
In 2014, an African American woman
who had a serious problem with her car rang
someone's doorbell to get help,
only to be shot and killed
by the man who opened the door.

RITES OF PASSAGE

Positions call out to us as if there were
ladders in our daily lives, and to reach
the upper rungs often means

listening to a person in order to use
her thoughts, but the thoughts keep rising
in that person like a spring

in the midst of a meadow. This is one
of the constant stories of our lives,
either to become prominent

and celebrated, or to turn away
from ladders to see roses
blooming on fences, how miniature

wild flowers rise from the cracks
of an asphalt road, to listen to the water
cascading over centuries

of serrated rocks that place us
in the center of creation, a monarch butterfly
alighting on a blade of grass,

for in the vast expanse
of the universe, enmity pales
and we are all just blades of grass.

QUESTION
for Barbara Schaff

How do you paint air?
Presence that announces itself
by what it is not,

the moonlight floating
in the ocean or a hawk
tracing the currents in slow arcs?

It drapes the shoulders of a woman
bent over her garden, fills
the empty glass on the windowsill.

It announces itself on a pond
splashing its yellows and greens.
It renders tempests,

in hot indigos and purples
racing above the bay,
holds blades of light

falling like sheet metal
on the rock-studded shore.
How do you paint air?

Think of tatters of smoke hanging
over streets after a war,
the sky weeping.

CEREMONIES

The shot rang out, ricocheting against the green,
catching the goose in mid-air.
Then, to our astonishment, a sudden gathering
of geese circles over and over the body
before landing and standing watch.
After, one of them steps out
slowly turning away, with the others
following in procession, wrapped in the dignity
of leave- taking, of a ceremony
honoring the fallen. They live and die
in freedom, journeying above
our noise and confusion,
unlike us, who say we live
in the land of the free, but who cannot gather
and mourn over our soldiers from
Iraq because the president has forbidden
public view of the coffins
that arrive in quick succession,
as he stakes out a silence that smothers us
and we obediently fold our wings.

THE WAY OF OUR CONTINUING
for Preston Hood

After the cyclone, life
and death merge; fields of uprooted
trees lying in heaps, closed
roads, yet on another slope
living trees overwhelm us

with their presence, enfolding
us in their power of being,
rising with the clouds
behind them, holding the meadow
in its roots, grazing sheep,

and their shapes, colors and sizes,
hold the beauty of a night sky, the pale
greens of becoming, the noise
of a plane no more than a wasp
or a dragonfly. Life and death

contain eternity. My friend
who returned from the war in
Vietnam with so many inner
scars, who used to run every
morning to outpace his demons,

now meditates, uses his pen
to create music from a history
of loss. Life and death merge
inside us and what we make
of it can be wondrous.

BOTH

can live together; heavy clouds
create an opening for sunshine,
the twittering birds fill
the air. But in Hong Kong
the heavy crowds...two million,
are but a moment, their voices
stilled by one person, and behind
her the person who holds
the reins of prison, silence, torture,
and acquiescence, but they can't
eliminate history, voices
that were flags, memories
that time cannot obliterate, Tiananmen
Square, the Tank Man,
the Umbrella Movement in 2014.
Beneath layers of lies, truth is a tree
that towers above barbed wire.

FORGIVENESS
in memory of Eva Kor

Sagittarius A, that astronomers
describe as a gravitational monster
pulled in passing stars in its
cosmic dance. Yet some stars manage

to survive the gravitational dance
of a black hole. Like Eva Kor
who survived Auschwitz because
she and her sister were treated

as guinea pigs by Dr. Mengele
who carried out his medical experiments
to create an Aryan master race.
She responded to the horrors by preaching

the power of forgiveness, persuading
a former physician at Auschwitz
to sign a document acknowledging
the gas chamber. Afterwards, Eva

wrote him a letter expressing her belief
in forgiving tormentors, and as
a thank you for his gesture, lifting
her burden of pain. We don't need

houses of worship to feel close
to the Creator, or astronomers
to explain the human cosmos,
but to face evil, the lust for power,

a hatred for others, and to respond
with a luminous soul rising
above the gravitational dance
of dark and light.

THE LAST WORD

In England and the United States
people hunt as a sport, but in the U.S.
guns are part of our culture.
But what do we mean when we say

our culture? In El Paso and Ford Bend
Texas, a county of 118 languages,
where people mingle with Mexicans
across the border, where according

to the President *A wall will protect us*
from Mexican rapists and dirty criminals,
but a gunman from "our culture" killed
22 people, and wounded 24 who were

rushed to a distant hospital. But the grief,
sorrow and shock created a language that
encompasses us all, a steeple of love; *the pain*
belongs to all of El Paso, and a woman prayed

for the gunman, *We don't want to be*
hateful, we want to forgive people.
Prayer circles came together, there was
music, dancing, flags of the U.S. and Mexico

fluttered together reminding us that we are
one family, like the man who lost his wife
and had no one else was comforted
by hundreds of people. There were flowers, candles,

but no borders, no walls, just a handwritten
poster, *Through the darkness light will prevail.*

GOYA'S ETCHINGS

At a time when truth is under
assault, crowds stream and disperse,
beneath his poignant etchings,
under the blade of his vision,
where centuries have unfurled
with wars, the rise and fall
of classes, sects and cultures,
the foibles we overlook,
such as greed, indifference,
the inability to perceive what
takes place before us because
we are too busy with our own
needs and desires, while an etching
entitled The Sleep of Reason
is a reminder, and one of an old man
standing over an open book
is titled with He Knows Much
But is Still Learning.

GESHE

Opening a book about Dharamsala, a distant
country and another way of life, I see
a portrait of a Buddhist monk, a Geshe,
a doctor of philosophy, looking out at me,
his face radiating calm, peace
and the knowledge that we pass by, both
in schools and in seminaries.
From the doorway of his damp, cold
and bare hut where he meditates,
his face emanates a holiness that is inclusive,
a richness of spirit that rises above
our shadows, our petty quarrels, our hunger
for power and material wealth, untouched
by the passage of time, war and
enmity, surrounding us with warmth,
and the depths of his understanding.

FAITH

Kazi Mannan, an immigrant
from Pakistan where he lived
in poverty, yet with a mother
who was always helping
people, now owns a restaurant
that is thriving, just a few blocks
away from the White House,
and gives free meals to the homeless
every day, reminding us
that Faith is in our action,
not just sitting in a mosque
or in a church.

The Earth's Scriptures

VOICES

The rhythmic thunderous roar
of the ocean pounding a long stretch
of bare sand, with no umbrellas or
fancy beach chairs covered with towels,

no trays of iced tea and coffee,
just the cliffs rising in their nakedness,
holding eons, and the layers
of clouds drifting by on their own

journey, and the damp sand
clinging to our bare feet, a skin
we have forgotten, and the ocean
clanging with a power we no longer

fathom, and the voices surrounding us
with their language of being and
becoming, silencing us, telling us
to reflect on our beginnings.

THE EMPEROR'S FORBIDDEN CITY

The palace holds ages of calligraphy,
hand wrought wood furniture,
gilded paintings that illuminate

the walls, panels of clouds populated
with otherworldly denizens, the stilled waves
of its many roofs. But time is also

beyond our measure, the earth speaking
its own languages, the epochs
of trees' vast calligraphies written

in their own twisted and intertwined
barks, its myriad of shapes curved
in all directions as the scriptures

of wind and water. Even the doorways
are set among layers of uncut
jutting rocks that are also carved

by eons, a firmament that outlasts
our history and knowledge, a wilderness
where sacredness dwells.

IN A SECLUDED COVE

beyond Poela Bay, Naupaka, creeping vine
with its maze of bark like stems,
gleaming white buds, holds
the volcanic and granite rocks
that rise above the clanging ocean,
covers up the flotsam dumped
by the heavy surf, keeping water
in its leaves in time of drought
and traveling in waves over the mountains
as the earth that is laid bare
changes, and turns on its molten
core, its story humming
around us that will outlast the jeeps
and trucks on winding roads,
those who build fires at night
leaving empty bottles
and trash behind them,
the wet cement of the highways.

PERSPECTIVES

In a world of vast cumulus clouds,
warming seas filled with the sting
of jellyfish, in a world of deeper stings
when a policeman shoots an innocent

black man, and then claims that he was just
protecting himself, where we do not see
ourselves in the "other," and are blinded by
hatred and a twisted version of history,

there is another world, a drawing of flowers
made by a four-year-old child, the hand
reaching out to another, the scent of a hidden
garden; sage, basil, thyme, the spurt

of bushes growing out of ancient
volcanic rock, green feathers growing
out of destruction, nature talking back
to us, love sliding through crevices.

MEETING IN WEST MAUI
for Maulupe Ofa

Sometimes   a word is   too small
too insignificant   like the word   smile
that cannot hold   the layers   of years
and understanding   the harmony
of sitting beneath   a tree that has its
own language   the land   they took away
from your people   that didn't take   its memories
or its history   the hands carving a wooden turtle
that will fly   on its own   journey   the eyes
that look   at a stranger   with ripples
of peace   and contentment   the grace
of a summer sky

SMALL MIRACLES

In a world that has lost its rhythms
of wind and air currents, the language
of clouds, all the threads
that entwine us, forests whose

winds send moisture to
dry lands, the ocean, a world
that has gone astray with its
rising temperature,

a bush of vibrant purple flowers
shimmers in an empty field,
and in Vacubo Puerto Rico,
on a seaside cliff where hurricane

Maria landed exactly a year ago,
a man with a sonorous voice
opens the day at sunrise
streaming it throughout the island,

"I am the light of the morning
that shines new paths,
that floods the mountains
and peasant trails."

LOOK ABOVE US

The mountain slope is dwarfed
 by the passage of massive clouds,
 moving in different directions and
continually changing shapes; the smaller ones
that are transparent soar upwards like spume
from behind the dense, furling waves
that have taken over the sky. The Alps' tallest
peaks seem miniature as if the wind
were telling us a story about dimensions;
the size of a speeding truck, an open
page in a book, a clump of soaring pines,
are like moments in time, and
that transcendence and mystery
are part of our lives.

NEIGHBORS

My neighbors on this mountain slope
are families of goats and sheep
that travel in waves, their tinkling bells
part of their language. They are busy
foraging tender blades of grass,
and when the sun is scalding,
they lie down together beneath
a tree. If they sense a storm brewing,
they gather again for shelter; black goats
and brown, a white goat speckled
with brown, the same for sheep, a communal
bond. They don't dream of large chalets,
of a made up splendor that sets us apart
from each other. Their steps are gentle
and they know how closely they are
intertwined with the land. Their paths
do not wound it, like the cranes,
and bulldozers that crowd the region
but help it retain its green lights,
and if their passage is brief,
it leaves no scars.

BECOMING NEW

As I clambered up the slopes
in late afternoon, light blazed
in my eyes, meadows
of green flames washed the air.
But in the clearing an old man
was standing motionless,
gazing at the snowy peaks
as if wings quivered deep
within his stolid shoulders,
as if the weight of his years
hadn't diminished him
but honed his ears
to the language of silence
and immensity, prepared him to see
as if for the first time.

DESPITE US

1
A cluster of glowing lilies rise in an abandoned
lot with a boarded house.

2
A leafy bush grows out of the top of limestone
rocks, its branches reaching out like palms
raised in halleluiahs.

3
A cedar tree carries centuries in its curved
trunks, with its own language, beyond
the tumult of passing cars and motorcycles.

4
Flowers that sprouted by themselves,
carry sun and sky; morning glories and nasturtiums
--scattered along the lower edges of jagged
bushes and left-behind behind objects,--
worlds within worlds in their nectar.

DAWN ON A FARAWAY ISLAND

The air is stitched together
by bird song, confounding
distance, the slow motion of leaves

on soaring palm trees, the green
rivers of Norfolk pines. Here
there are no headlines of violence

and misdeeds in so many different
places. Here everything is intertwined;
the quiet music of soil, of buds

with the promise of scent and color
that enfolds us, ferns, bushes
and even trees rising from

the eloquent lime stone, its striations
and ridged surfaces with
so many openings, speaking

of presence and plenitude
where spirit prevails,
the radiance of untethered light.

A DREAM OF ORDER

There is a new word that speaks of our presence,
polar vortex. It is weakening and sometimes split
in two leaving snow on a row of gondoliers in Venice,
unexpected storms in Scotland and England,

but we are too busy with a crew of workers
felling a stretch of white pines, another one
delves deep into the soil to prepare
for the pouring of cement. But despite

the bitter cold, a bird with its two note song
calls out -- the voice of the embattled
earth, of wave upon wave of undulating
grass in the meadow, of wildflowers

on the breast of a high mountain just above
the boom of chalets, the music of migrating geese,
their old alignments of motion and grace,
of wonder and the holy practice of balance.

THERE WAS ONCE A SEA

of green in the mountains,
its tall blades undulating in the wind
with its seeds glittering in waves,
purple, yellow, dark and light
blue flowers glisten
and the sea is not contained,
but rises through the asphalt
on its own trajectory,
a journey whose sounds
are not crashing waves,
but crickets, clanging bells,
hidden streams. There were
once farmers whose blood
pulsed with these sounds,
the tides of fallow and fullness,
It was a world in which
we were one with the earth
that we worshiped
and tended its many gifts.

SIMULTANEOUSLY

In Sistiana, Italy, the temperatures
soar to the high nineties, and in France
above one hundred. Then in the French Alps
where the melèzes and other pine trees

flourish and have been towering
above the houses and construction,
carrying centuries, oxygen, and water
in their beings, a cyclone that never

occurs in these mountains felled
many hundreds of them leaving
blocked roads, a war zone,
that we quietly initiated

with our daily actions, lack
of attention, and our deliberate
insistence that we are on the top
of the scales of importance,

ignoring the warnings of scientists,
while a woman in New York
city has quietly created an exhibit
of how plants speak to each

other through their vibrations
that can be captured in audios
awakening us to the depth
and complexity of the creation.

THE IMPORTANCE OF FLOWERS
for Pascale

After the cyclone, rows of felled trees
lie in front of the apartment building

and then there are the stumps,
that leave a message of destruction,

but the caretaker of the buildings
has placed a pot of magnificent

flowers on each stump, each one
with its own bloom and color

giving another message,
one written by the famous Buddhist

Thich Nhat Hanh, one flower
is made of the whole cosmos.

HARMONY

The ostrich can sense lions
from great distances, undulating like water
as she speeds through the bush.
The wisest of birds

she outwits her predators
by laying her head and neck
on the ground until her body
becomes part of the brush and haze.

She protects her chicks by leading
marauders away from the nest
in ever widening circles,
uses her powerful legs

as weapons when cornered.
There are people who pen her
behind wire where she is bruised
by stares, people who have forgotten

how the land flows past singing her stories.
Ethiopians still place ostrich eggs
on the roofs of their churches
to grace them, the Dogon believe

the ostrich is embodied light.
We live in a web of plants, trees,
animals, stars -- the earth
whose skin is our own.

EARTH'S SCRIPTURES

Along a walk by the lake in Lausanne
I pass a cedar tree from the Atlas Mountains

in Africa it's massive trunk rippling with
waves of bark, the way it holds light

and shadow, the fire of its colors and
its being, its branches rising

skyward and gathering it in,
its presence the earth's cassock,

its guardian, its silence carrying eons
in its arms, awakening us to reverence.

DIMENSIONS

The mountain rises above the slopes,
and villages, erasing distances,
accompanied by clouds,
but on the wire that stretches
before our window a tiny
bird perches every evening
claiming its right.

THE THERMAL PARK AT LE FAYET

On one side, a river flows among
a multitude of rocks, the water
spurting over them in so many
directions, emerging from thousands
of years through underground
rocks, and the heights of the Mont Blanc,
with its persistent and calming
music, with its stones and their
minerals singing. And on the other
side, ancient cedar trees whose trunks
are foundations stitching earth
and sky. Water, rocks, trees,
sheltering prisms of clean air
a million heartbeats.

TWO WORLDS

There are the morning newspapers
with stories of war, corruption
and political strife, but there are also
the evergreens rising towards

the sky, enfolding us in their scent
and majesty, despite the steady
rumble of construction behind them,
gouging the earth and transforming

greed into progress. But there is
something called hope with
a million translations; the Mt. Blanc
which was once reduced to barren rock

is now covered with a fresh mantle
of snow, and by the road leading
to the parking lot, a shimmering
green field is aflame with buttercups,

and below the clouds towering
above, the buildings and roads
are but a grain of sand in the endless
cycle of creation.

PERCEPTION

There is the should, of our daily lives
in what seems like an endless
list of chores, and the would, we all
hunger for, like the fauve painter Manguin

whose vibrant colors glimmered
not just in trees and flowers,
but in our faces and bare arms
at one with the sea's glitter at high noon,

the unexpected lights among
shadows, the flames of a scarf
draped behind a chair, the sinuous
branches weaving it all together,

and how dreaming brings us
closer to the reality that drowns
when we look at our watches
and rush through time.

WHERE EVERYTHING HAPPENS

PARIS

The guardians of Paris carry hundreds
of years in the bark of soaring
plane trees. Lindens hold the sky

in their branches, unveil tapestries
of leaves, and the delicate, refined
stone of the buildings, the balconies'

wrought iron lace, the intricately
carved doors, and the centuries
in the church's naves, pages

of one of the many versions
of history. And on the streets,
the ones that are being written,

pushing all the Roma outside
the borders, wanting them to be
impermeable -- the little girl

with long black hair
who was begging at the railroad
station who never harmed

a soul -- . and the bridges
where elegance walks by
in high heels, fluttering scarves,

her perfume lingering, unaware
of the people sleeping nearby
on the ground rolled up in blankets,

with small bundles at their side –
the pages of vision, accomplishment,
conflict, hope and despair.

BEHIND THE CHURCH

In the garden behind St. Julien Le Pauvre
a Melkite church on a small Parisian
street, a massive tree planted
in the sixteenth century
bows towards the ground where memories
are stored in its roots, wreathes
of leaves converse with the light.
It too is a chapel -- with no
icons or effigies, but where wings
visit us and the striations
on its bark are a living book
reminding us that it
has overcome the weather,
the tempest of events
and migrations -- that we are not
the center of the world.

LA ROUTE DE MAISON NEUVE

Where the road curves upward
is a tiny house, balanced on the slope
above the town spreading
up the mountain.
There is a small garden in front,
clumps of old fashioned flowers,
a lacy wrought iron cross
rises above a stone pedestal
with flower boxes on either side.
Could it be for a child
who has died or homage
to the Creator? When it is warm
an elderly couple sit before
an open door. The room
is just big enough for a table
covered with oil cloth.
They do not wave or smile
as we pass by, conversing
by their thoughts. We can read
in their faces that life
is more than living,
that what matters is not
the shuttered elegant chalets
that line the upper road, but this place
where everything happens.

LETTER TO MY DAUGHTER

Like the crimson flamboyants
burning on a leafless tree,
things I never told you
bloom inside me.
I want to praise the arduous steps
you climb inside your heart,
the courage that made you choose life,
when it came at such a high cost,
that made you carve your name
in a country that tries to dismiss
you as just another stranger
even though you've lived there
for years. I want to celebrate
your singular light glowing
amidst the turbulent flux of events,
and how you stride through the pain
of indifference in a world
where some are born
to walk with ease,
and some are born hemmed in
by brambles yet dancing.

ARIEL

My teenage granddaughter's smile
is like a stained glass window,

luminescent with its greens,
rose, and amethysts, its myriad

of colors where the story
of the blessed life spills out

through the window panes;
kindness and generosity

to every passerby;
the lesson that difficult times

are part of our journey
and that real light comes

from within like the sky
opening at daybreak.

GOYA'S PORTRAIT

Maria Antonia Gonzaga,
the Marchioness of Villafranca, steps
out of the frame and enters

our space, engaging us with her presence
because she has so much
to tell us about life; the importance

of reflection on what is taking place
around us, her experience
of the dark moments

in her time, and the search
for meaning. She lost her son
the Duke of Alba, and although surrounded

by people of standing, she lives
alone with her memories and her deep
thoughts. What she acquired

over the years are neither her high position,
which spares no one, nor the jewels
and silks that adorn her,

but the importance of understanding,
how to carry the weight
of the world with grace.

UNSPOKEN

There is so much I want to say
to my cousin's daughter Cristiana,
who is dying of cancer; that the scarf
I brought her to cover her bald head
is insignificant because her high intelligence,
and her courage still blooms when
she goes out and ignores the stares
at her head and almost skeletal body,
that the love and caring she gave
her children over the years
are precious gifts that will always be
with them, and make them strong
and self-confident, so that they will
grow in new ways throughout their lives,
and that love doesn't disappear but will
always flame in our hearts after
she has traveled beyond this world.

NO WORDS

for Valentino

can hold your sorrow for watching
a daughter take her last
breath, who was the center
of your life for decades,

whom you cared for day and night
while she was battling
cancer, her long black hair
disappearing like spring flowers,

her smile erased, arms that held
her two children, the wings
of her courage and intelligence.
There is supposed to be a calendar

in our journey through the years,
with the older leaving the path
for the younger, with parents
caring for their children.

Now you have no words, you who
were in charge of the radar on ships
that brought you throughout
the world where you felt as one

with the ocean and now
you face traveling through alien days
with no radar, no compass
for the inexplicable ocean of life.

JUST WORDS

When my Italian cousin Sandro was recovering
from a heart attack and craving forbidden

cigarettes, the gift I gave him with a hug
was how to swear in four languages

just so he could journey
to another country without the baggage

of pain, the limp from the prosthesis
after a second bout with cancer.

But that was only a quick flight,
for he has his own wings, his intricate

and delicate drawings,
constellations radiating in a dark sky.

IN ONLY ONE NIGHT

The mountain of San Simeon
shuddered from its roots: Gemona
lay shattered, its piazzas
streets, memories crushed
in barely a minute.

Who would know it today?
Not the caffé with its tables and parasols
or the storefronts glittering with jewelry
or the artist with her brush poised
over a newly fired bowl.

Not the stone monks at the entrance
of the church in their worn cloaks and hoods,
as if neither centuries
nor earthquakes could lure them
from their devotions.

Not the dove tracing its white arc
in the tympanum.

LESSONS

Where the slopes open their pages
of light and shadow,
and rocks are jumbled together
like the bones of our past,

the lessons still dangle before me.
I see Miss Durgin leading us
through the foreign country
of Shakespeare, when the dust

on the windowpanes seemed
more eloquent and the minute hands
were weighted down. As I gouged
my name on the desk, Miss Durgin,

her face lit with inexplicable joy,
told us that literature would be there
someday when we needed a window.
In late afternoon the peaks dissolve

into a luminous smoky blue.
In the mountains I am scaling
the earth of myself, journeying
through illness.

I'm in Somalia, lying on my side
with a bloated belly,
in Dubrovnik, waiting in line
for water. My body ushers me

to the blood-stained wedding
where I finally marry the world.

DIAGNOSIS

The physician's name has the music
of Greek but he does not use it
nor does he use mine,
because I am a file
that passes through his hands
like a leaf in the wind,
and he is a man of few words.
"Your memory will not return,"
he tells me as if he were enunciating
the details in his hands.
His eyes are for glances
that move as quickly
as the leaves. He does not see
what is behind my quiet face;
the breadth and depth of a
rich life. He does not know that
even if the left lobe in the brain
is "permanently damaged"
the heart can hold the world.

MOMENTS

During what seemed like endless hours
in a physician's waiting room
I spoke with an assistant who was Indian
about the breadth and precision

of different languages, shared jokes
with a woman who had waited to be seen
even longer then me, grumbled
to myself that I hadn't remembered

to bring a book. Then, I saw a heavy set
woman in her late thirties who was like
a child of ten, stepping out of an
examination room with her elderly mother

who was trying to calm her terror
of an impending operation. I walked over
to her, held her in my arms, telling her
that it's all right to be afraid and sad.

She showed me her large key chain
with a cross attached she held for comfort.
While she wept I stroked her hair.
Then, as I walked away, she called out

Thank you, I don't know your faith
but you will go to heaven, teaching me that
the heart has its own wisdom, how life is made
of moments that belie the weight of hours.

PESIRA

At the airport, a megalopolis crowd churns by,
each person or family intent on their destination,
the minutes and hours guiding their steps.
A woman pushes my wheelchair to the gate.
She is quiet, steady in her task, her face taut,
withdrawn, but I ask her where she is from
because the cloud of her hair and her accent
speaks of a distant world. "I am from Africa "
she states. "Where in Africa?" I continue.
"Kenya, why did you ask?" she queries
with suspicion. As we go through security,
the chair is examined by an irritable guard
with an electric wand, and she is criticized.
I watch her shrug her shoulders
as if she were casting off the dailiness
of her trials. Then on the ramp to the plane,
I tell her I didn't mean to be rude
with my questions, believing that everyone
is a story. She leans over and whispers,
"My name is Pesira. What is yours?"
"Marguerite," I reply, seeing her face pulse
with an inner light that follows me
with its glow as we hold each other
across so many boundaries,
redeeming ourselves from invisibility.

TWO MAKE ONE

On a bench at the exit
of a hospital sit a white haired man
with one arm around his wife's

shoulders and the other holding
her hand, both of them vibrating
with tenderness, carrying

so many years, days, and hours
of good and painful times.
People pass them by

without noticing that in a small
corner there is a universe of our
humanity -- while we dispute

destiny, fate, different perspectives --
the world is held together
not by success or possessions,

but when we find ourselves
in another person and discover
that love is boundless.

ANOTHER WAY

Those who want glory, do not wish
to see themselves in need,
forgetting that our time
on this earth is brief

and what fills it are a child's
laughter, a river of tears,
the touch of hands, the book
of days we signed with our moments

of joy and sorrow intertwined,
a ray of sunshine piercing the clouds,
your loved one's presence,
for love is what holds our world

together when it shatters into
different zones, is what carries us
through the turbulence
of our times. Look closely at what

surrounds you, for darkness
and light co-exist, and the light
has so many different voices,
that echo in your heart.

AUTUMN

My Japanese maple is a symphony
of light, not just the tender blaze
of springtime. It sings adagio,
lento, the turning of time
and all that it holds; the deep
glow of a long marriage,
the house that we built
together that wears our
signatures, my travels
over so many paths, and
through difficult times, learning
the grace of pain, and how
it connects you to so many
troubled places in our world,
the deep glow of a life
well lived.

A DIFFERENT WAY OF SEEING

Do we look at the sky during
our hectic days, or slow down
to the world of silence?
We believe that visions

appear just in holy books
but never happen to mere
mortals, yet Odilon Redon
combines light and darkness

in many different ways, the astral
and the earthly; in a cerulean
sky, a face with luminous
wings with a wave of gleaming

flowers behind it, the star light
of our daily lives, a couple
seated close together in a boat
whose love is not hemmed

in by their bodies that are vibrant
and luminous. We all have visions
when we least expect them.
When I was meditating before

a journey into danger after the demise
of a military junta, I saw myself
standing in a train holding a strap
hanging from a band of light,

and while my cousin's daughter was
in the harsh white of a hospital,
in Italy, a flame suddenly quenched,
I saw a swirl of light rising upwards.

Like Odilon Redon if we open our inner
eyes to all that cannot be contained
by time or place there is an intertwining
of the astral and the earthly.

THE GIFT

Forget the wires stretching between
        ski lifts, another world
that is now silenced with only the
        twittering of birds,
their quiet music. What reigns here
        are stately evergreens
birches and ash, the scattering of wildflowers
        that are white caps
on the river of grass, with clouds, sky
        and meadow intertwined.
They are not silent, but murmuring
        inside us, a presence
that was here before us, with no doors,
        only windows into our
hearts, minds, and souls where time and
        timelessness coexist.

THE BOOK OF LIGHTS

We like to measure time;
hours, days, and decades of our

passage that hold our brief
stories, but our travels through its

burgeoning traffic just
dissolve as we stand before

the murmuring ocean at dusk,
with lights spanning the vast circle

of sky; deep orange, layers of rose,
golden streaks intertwining

with shimmering clouds, pale blues,
its changing calligraphy,

telling us that eternity holds us
in our inner beings.

Marguerite Guzmán Bouvard has published over 22 books, including eleven books of poetry as well as books on human rights, women's rights, social justice, illness and grief. Her poetry and essays have been widely anthologized and her poetry books have won the Quarterly Review of Literature Award and the MassBook Award for Poetry. She has received grants for her poetry from the Puffin and Danforth Foundations. One of her poems has won a prize from Writing in A Woman's Voice, and two of her poems and books have been featured in the Blue Mesa Press.

She is currently working on a non-fiction book, Physicians and Nurses On the Frontline of the Pandemic. She sees a similarity to the book she wrote some years ago, "The Invisible Wounds of War; Coming Home From Iraq and Afghanistan," because too many of us just want to get out, go to restaurants, and have a good time, forgetting the heroes and heroines who are surrounded by the seriously ill, and so many deaths.

Made in the USA
Columbia, SC
14 March 2021

34484345R00052